Discovering People

DISCOVERING PEOPLE

NEEPIN AUGER

RMB

Baby

bébé

oskawâsis

Me

moi

niya

Mother

mère

okâwîmâw

Father

père

ohtâwiy

Grandmother

grand-mère

ôhkom

Grandfather

grand-père

mosôm

Sister

sœur

nîtisân

Brother

frère

nîtisân

nikâwîs

Auntie

tante

ohcâwîsimâw

Uncle

oncle

enseignant(e)

Teacher

okiskinohamâkêw

étudiant(e)

Student

okiskinohamawâkan

maskihkîwiyiniw

médecin

Doctor

maskihkîwiskwêw

Nurse

infirmier/-ière

Police Officer

simâkanis

policier/-ière

sapeur-pompier

otâstawêhikêw

Firefighter

kâ-wîcihimât maskihkîwiyiniw

Paramedic

auxiliaire médical(e)

kâ-onanâtawihowêw pisiskiwak

vétérinaire

Veterinarian

danseur/-euse

onîmihitow

Dancer

Drummer

batteur(e)

kâ-takahkwêwêhtitâw

maskihkîwiskwêw

Medicine Woman

femme de
médecine

maskihkîwiyiniw

Medicine Man

homme de
médecine

Pronunciation Guide

Baby	bébé	oskawâsis	
	bay-bay	oskuwaasis	
Me	moi	niya	
	mwa	neeyu	
Mother	mère	okâwîmâw	
	mair	okaaweemaaw	
Father	père	ohtâwiy	
	pair	ohtaaweey	

	Grandmother	grand-mère	ôhkom
		gron-mair	oohkom
	Grandfather	grand-père	mosôm
		gron-pair	mosoom
	Sister	sœur	nîtisân
		ser	neetisaan
	Brother	frère	nîtisân
		frair	neetisaan
	Auntie	tante	nikâwîs
		tont	nikaawees
	Uncle	oncle	ohcâwîsimâw
		on-cl-euh	ohtsaaweesimaaw

Teacher   enseignant/-ante   okiskinohamâkêw
[masculine-feminine]
on-sen-ya / on-sen-yont   okiskinohumaakayoo

Student   étudiant/-ante   okiskinohamawâkan
[masculine-feminine]
eh-too-dee-ya / eh-too-dee-yont   okiskinohumuwaakun

Doctor   médecin   maskihkîwiyiniw
med-san   muskeehkeeweeyinoo

Nurse   infirmier/-ière   maskihkîwiskwêw
[masculine-feminine]
an-fer-mee-ay / an-fer-mee-air   muskeehkeewiskwayoo

Police Officer   policier/-ière   simâkanis
[masculine-feminine]
po-lees-ee-ay / po-lees-ee-air   simaakunis

Firefighter   sapeur-pompier   otâstawêhikêw
sap-euhr-pom-pee-ay   otaastuwayhikayoo

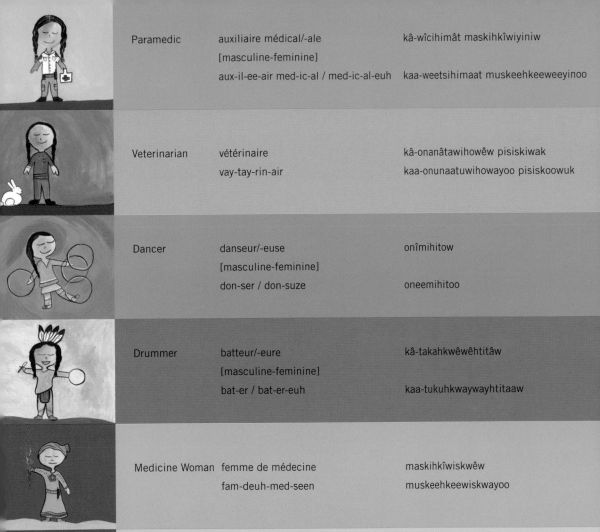

Paramedic	auxiliaire médical/-ale [masculine-feminine] aux-il-ee-air med-ic-al / med-ic-al-euh	kâ-wîcihimât maskihkîwiyiniw kaa-weetsihimaat muskeehkeeweeyinoo	
Veterinarian	vétérinaire vay-tay-rin-air	kâ-onanâtawihowêw pisiskiwak kaa-onunaatuwihowayoo pisiskoowuk	
Dancer	danseur/-euse [masculine-feminine] don-ser / don-suze	onîmihitow oneemihitoo	
Drummer	batteur/-eure [masculine-feminine] bat-er / bat-er-euh	kâ-takahkwêwêhtitâw kaa-tukuhkwaywayhtitaaw	
Medicine Woman	femme de médecine fam-deuh-med-seen	maskihkîwiskwêw muskeehkeewiskwayoo	
Medicine Man	homme de médecine om-deuh-med-seen	maskihkîwiyiniw muskeehkeeweeyinoo	

We would like to also take this opportunity to acknowledge the traditional territories upon which we live and work. In Calgary, Alberta, we acknowledge the Niitsitapi (Blackfoot) and the people of the Treaty 7 region in Southern Alberta, which includes the Siksika, the Piikuni, the Kainai, the Tsuut'ina and the Stoney Nakoda First Nations, including Chiniki, Bearpaw, and Wesley First Nations. The City of Calgary is also home to Métis Nation of Alberta, Region III. In Victoria, British Columbia, we acknowledge the traditional territories of the Lkwungen (Esquimalt, and Songhees), Malahat, Pacheedaht, Scia'new, T'Sou-ke and W̱SÁNEĆ (Pauquachin, Tsartlip, Tsawout, Tseycum) peoples.

For my daughter Gracie

For information on purchasing bulk quantities of this book, or to obtain media excerpts or invite the author to speak at an event, please visit rmbooks.com and select the "Contact" tab.

RMB I Rocky Mountain Books Ltd.
rmbooks.com
@rmbooks
facebook.com/rmbooks

Cataloguing data available from Library and Archives Canada
ISBN 9781771604710 (paperback)
ISBN 9781771603270 (board book)
ISBN 9781771603287 (electronic)

Cree translations and pronunciations by Naomi McIlwraith and Cree Elder Elizabeth Letendre
French translations and pronunciations by David Warriner
Book design by Chyla Cardinal

Printed and bound in China

We acknowledge the financial support of the Government of Canada through the Canada Book Fund and the Canada Council for the Arts, and of the province of British Columbia through the British Columbia Arts Council and the Book Publishing Tax Credit.

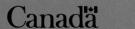